# EXCEPTIONAL EYE TRICKS

# EXCEPTIONAL EYE TRICKS

BRAD HONEYCUTT

imagine!
Publishing

An Imagine Book
Published by Charlesbridge
85 Main Street
Watertown, MA 02472
(617) 926-0329
www.charlesbridge.com

Library of Congress Control Number: 2012937972
ISBN 13: 978-1-936140-73-2

Printed in China. Manufactured in September, 2012.
(hc) 10 9 8 7 6 5 4 3 2 1

Designed by Cindy LaBreacht

For information about custom editions, special sales, premium and corporate purchases,
please contact Charlesbridge Publishing at specialsales@charlesbridge.com

**Dedicated to the memory of JERRY ANDRUS (1918-2007), visionary illusionist, skeptic, and magician.**

"I can fool you because you're a human. You have a wonderful human mind that works no different from my human mind. Usually, when we're fooled, the mind hasn't made a mistake. It's come to the wrong conclusion for the right reason."—JERRY ANDRUS

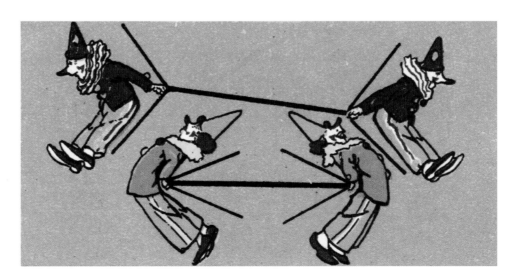

# CONTENTS

# INTRODUCTION

OPTICAL ILLUSIONS AND VISUAL PHENOMENA are everywhere—we are surrounded by them. Some, such as mirages, rainbows, and rock formations, occur naturally compliments of Mother Nature. Others are created by artists and scientists, either unintentionally or deliberately. Regardless of their origin, illusions have the ability to amuse, confuse, or fool the viewer. Illusions are also a good reminder that we do not see the world as it really exists, but rather as how we perceive it with our own eyes and biases.

The first optical illusion that I have a memory of is *L'egs-istential Quandary*, created by American psychologist Roger N. Shepard. This drawing is commonly known as the "Impossible Elephant" or the "Anomalous Elephant" for good reason. At first glance, it appears to be a simple black and white drawing of an elephant. Closer examination reveals that the feet at the bottom of the drawing do not match up with the animal's legs, creating an impossible situation that could certainly not exist in nature. Your mind tries to (and certainly wants to) make the feet line up, but it is no use. What makes this a classic optical illusion is that it can be thoroughly enjoyed by people of all ages. I was perplexed by this drawing as a child, and continue to marvel at it as an adult. As much as I've tried over the years, I still cannot get the feet to line up properly with the rest of the body. I suspect (and hope) that I never will.

This book contains optical illusions from a variety of different artists, researchers, and photographers. These images have been categorized into chapters based on illusion type. Many of the images in this book contain elements of two (or more) of these categories. A good example is Jerry Andrus' *Impossible Crate* (page 109), which is included in the Perspective Illusions chapter because the effect can only be seen from one particular vantage point. The construction of the crate itself also presents a seemingly "impossible" object, so this image would fit equally well in the Impossible Illusions chapter. It should be no surprise that the categorization of such deceptive material would prove to be ambiguous and subjective. Regardless of their assigned category, the optical illusions presented in this book will hopefully perplex you and bring a smile to your face simultaneously.

*Brad* —Brad Honeycutt

**L'EGS-ISTENTIAL QUANDARY** BY ROGER N. SHEPARD

# AMBIGUOUS
## ILLUSIONS

Some optical illusions are designed to be ambiguous so there are multiple (often two) meanings, depending on how the image is perceived. Sometimes, the viewer may not even recognize that a second meaning exists. Once this fact is pointed out or becomes known, however, both meanings become apparent simultaneously, and the viewer can often "flip-flop" between the two.

## ANGEL COLUMNS

Do you notice anything unique about these columns?

SEE PAGE 122 FOR THE SOLUTION AND ADDITIONAL INFORMATION.

## DANCE WITH ME

As a man and woman dance among the trees, an ominous face seems to be watching them.

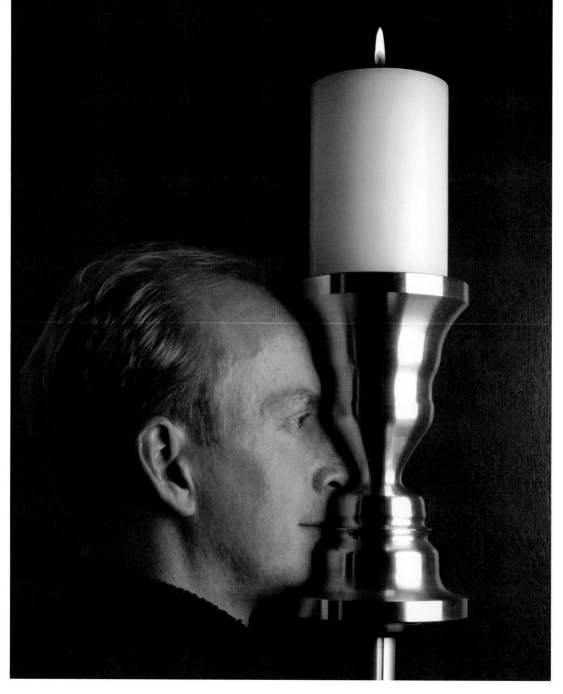

## METAL PORTRAIT

The profile of a man's face can be seen on this candlestick.

SEE PAGE 122 FOR THE SOLUTION AND ADDITIONAL INFORMATION.

## AMBIGUOUS CHEESE

Do you see a slab of cheese with a section cut out of it or a single, protruding slice of cheese?

SEE PAGE 122 FOR THE SOLUTION AND ADDITIONAL INFORMATION.

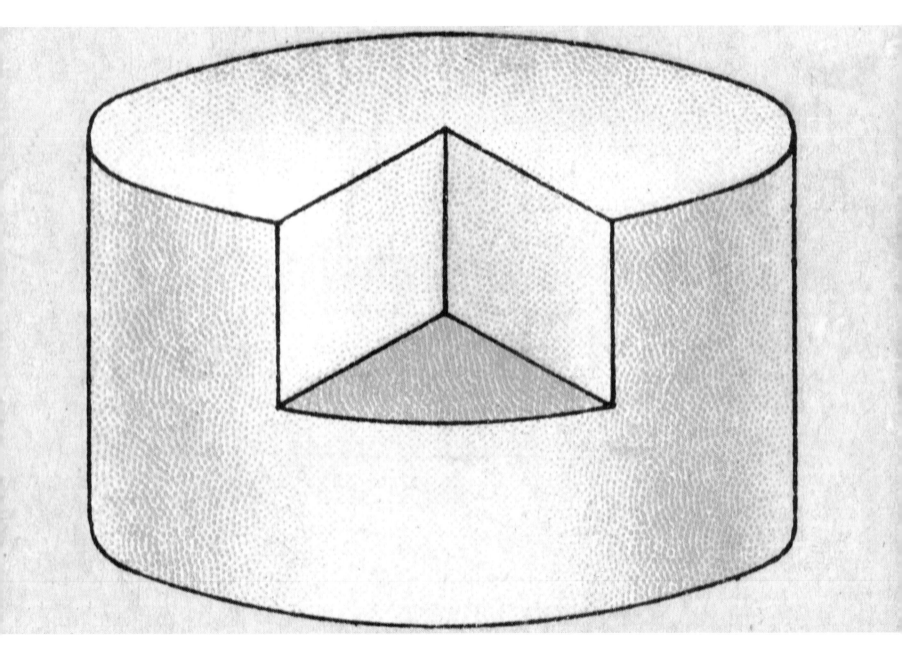

**I GOT A DEER**

This lion caught a deer
for dinner; can you find it?

SEE PAGE 122 FOR THE SOLUTION.

**THE GHOST
IN THE TOWER**

There are four
people in this scene.
Can you find them all?

SEE PAGE 122 FOR THE
SOLUTION AND ADDITIONAL
INFORMATION.

## NEGATIVE-SPACE AMBIGRAM

Do you see both words presented in this negative-space ambigram?

SEE PAGE 122 FOR THE SOLUTION AND ADDITIONAL INFORMATION.

## PERCEIVED OBJECTS

Do you perceive a triangle and a sphere?

SEE PAGE 122 FOR THE SOLUTION AND ADDITIONAL INFORMATION.

## ERNEST HEMINGWAY

Ernest Hemingway sits at his desk, writing under an overhead lamp. Can you find the alternate meaning of this illustration from graphic designer Tang Yau Hoong?

SEE PAGE 122 FOR THE SOLUTION.

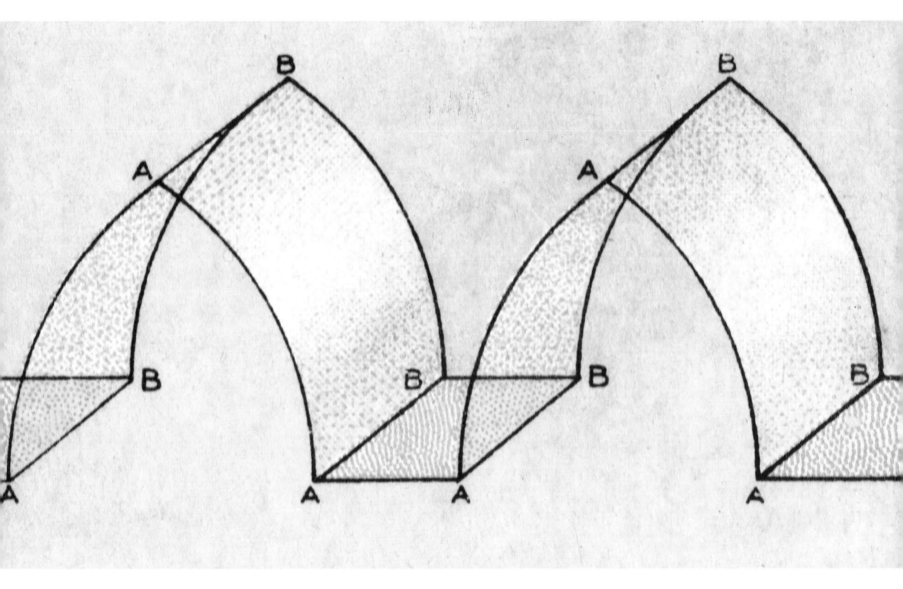

**CHANGING ARCHES**

The entrances to the two ambiguous archways can be perceived either through the openings AAA or BBB.

### THREE GRACES

A woman in a black dress can be seen standing between the two women facing each other.

**MAD OR SAD?**

Can you find portraits of a
man who looks mad and
a man who looks sad?

SEE PAGE 122 FOR THE SOLUTION.

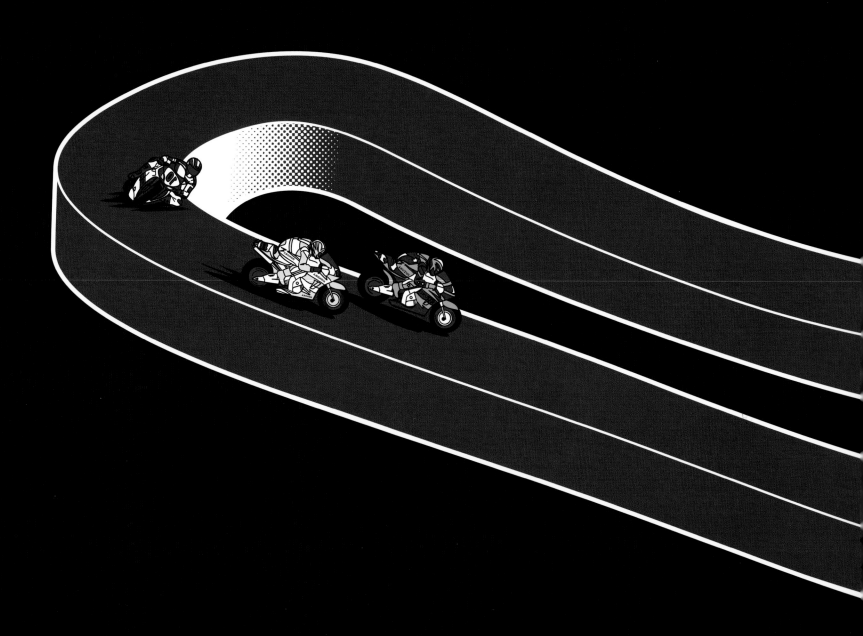

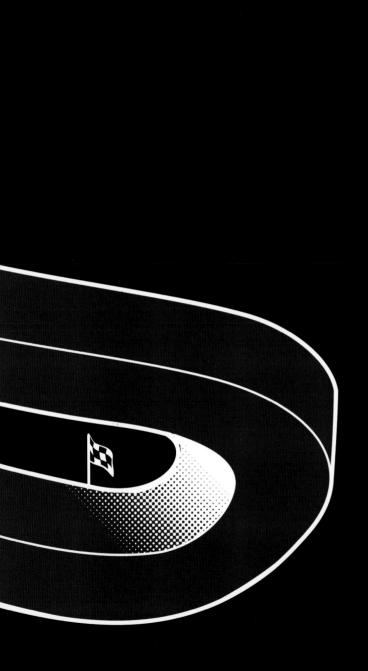

# IMPOSSIBLE
## ILLUSIONS

Impossible illusions consist of objects that are interpreted by the viewer as a three-dimensional figure that could not possibly exist in the real world. Even after the impossibility has been understood and acknowledged by a viewer, the objects still maintain the perception of being not physically possible. Artists, researchers, and mathematicians are all fascinated by these figures due to the contradictions between what is seen and what the brain processes.

Swedish artist Oscar Reutersvärd, who drew an impossible triangle in 1934, is credited with being the first person to intentionally design an impossible figure. Reutersvärd continued to draw these types of objects during his lifetime, amassing a collection of thousands of deceptive figures. He is often referred to as "the father of impossible figures" for his work in this area.

## BIZARRE DOGS

How many dogs do you see here?
Are you sure?

## D FOR DECEIVE

The person walking up
this staircase will be
surprised to discover
that they did not ascend
upon reaching the top.
Graphic designer
Tang Yau Hoong created
this deceptive scene.

## IMPOSSIBLE TRIANGLE

How is this triangle possible?

SEE PAGE 122 FOR THE SOLUTION AND ADDITIONAL INFORMATION.

## HIGHWAY
Photographer Michael Kai created this impossible scene where up is down and down is up.

SEE PAGE 122 FOR ADDITIONAL INFORMATION.

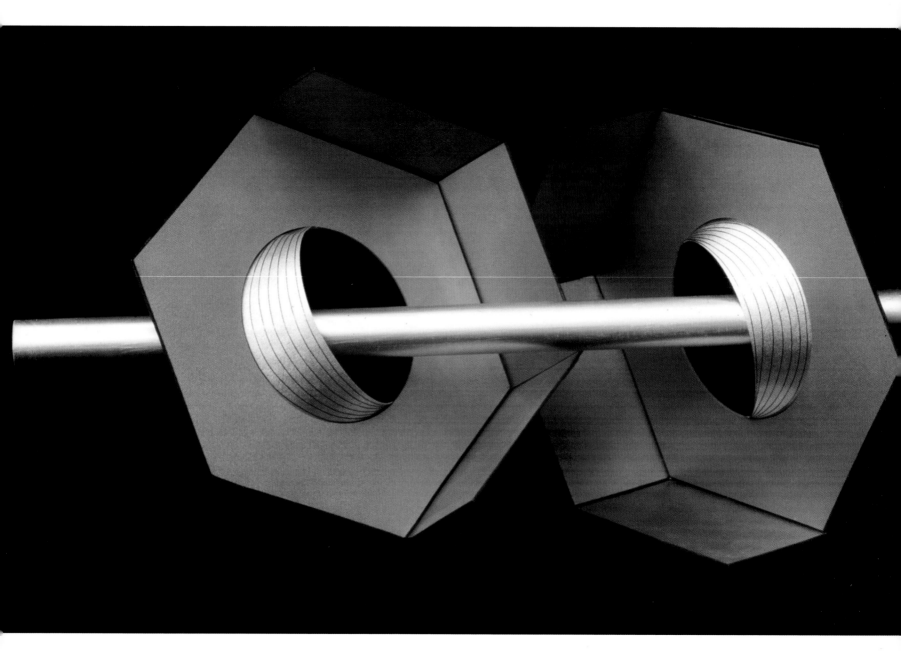

## IMPOSSIBLE NUTS

A straight bar appears to pass through two nuts facing different directions.

SEE PAGE 122 FOR THE SOLUTION AND ADDITIONAL INFORMATION.

## IMPOSSIBLE SPIRAL STAIRCASE

What is wrong with this staircase?

SEE PAGE 123 FOR THE SOLUTION AND ADDITIONAL INFORMATION.

**DIMENSION
II. IX FT**
Gold and silver
figures twist,
bend, and
intersect in
an impossible
manner in this
figure created
by geometric
artist Tamás
Farkas.

© 2011 Erwin Bomsma

## TOURIST TRAP II

Created in a bygone era, by a people long forgotten, using skills forever lost, the Tower at the World's Corner prominently stands at the corner of the world. Trespassing is allowed, but mind the step. Please make a donation before you enter.

SEE PAGE 123 FOR ADDITIONAL INFORMATION.

**IMPOSSIBLY LINKED**
These interlocking figures bend in ways that would not be physically possible.

**CHECKMATE**
Anyone care for a game of impossible chess?

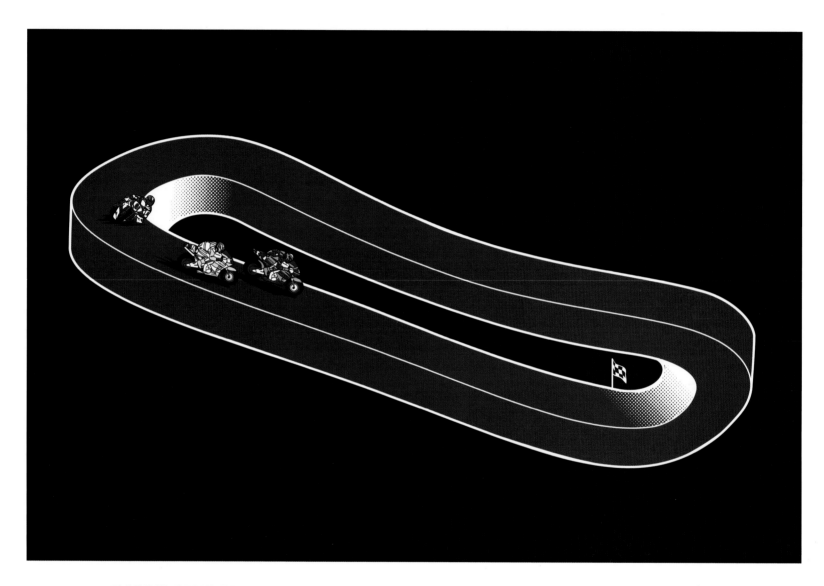

**RACING ILLUSION**

The three motorcycles will have difficulty completing their lap around this impossible racetrack.

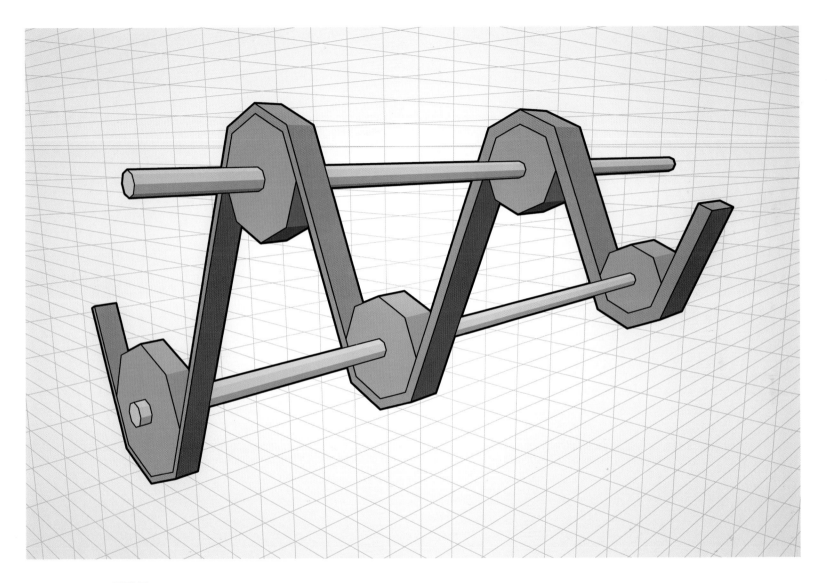

## BELT

The axles are angled away from you as a straight belt somehow connects all of the wheels.

SEE PAGE 123 FOR ADDITIONAL INFORMATION.

# COMPOSITE
## ILLUSIONS

Composite illusions are created by combining a series of smaller images or objects to form a larger portrait. This type of illusion was initially made popular in the 16th century by Italian painter Giuseppe Arcimboldo. One of his techniques was to paint portraits of people made from fruits, vegetables, and other objects. His work continues to influence modern-day artists.

## UNCLE SAM PHOTOGRAPHIC MOSAIC

This image of Uncle Sam is composed of more than 700 posters from World War I.

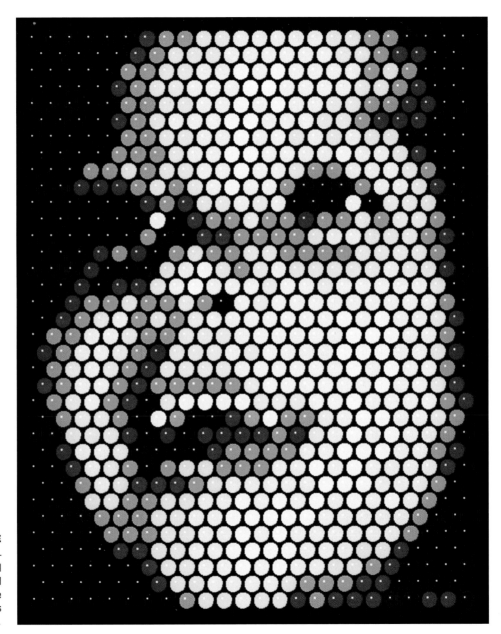

**STEPHANIE**

This computer-produced virtual portrait of M&M candies reveals the face of the artist's granddaughter.

**SUMMER**

A man's profile
emerges from
an assortment
of fully ripe fruits
and vegetables.

SEE PAGE 123 FOR
THE SOLUTION
AND ADDITIONAL
INFORMATION.

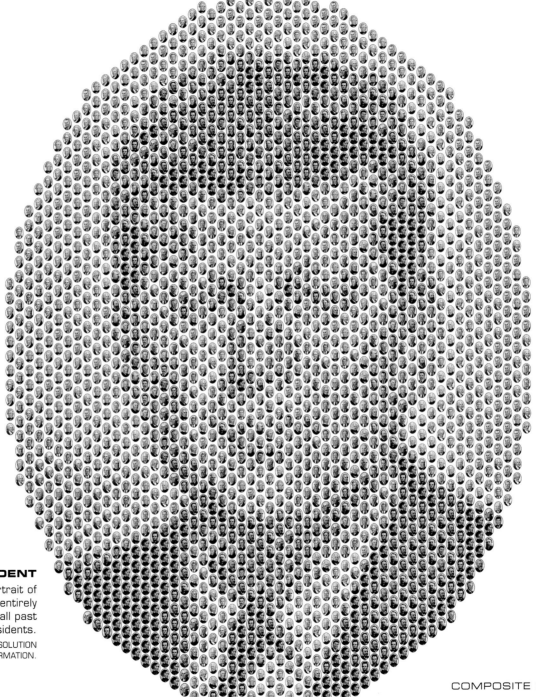

## PIXEL PRESIDENT

This presidential portrait of
John F. Kennedy is made entirely
from the portraits of all past
U.S. presidents.

SEE PAGE 123 FOR THE SOLUTION
AND ADDITIONAL INFORMATION.

**POST-IT NOTE ELVIS**

This tribute to Elvis Presley on a conference room wall was made with a popular office staple. See page 123 for the solution and additional information.

**PHOTOGRAPHIC MOSAIC**

This image of a trolley in Istanbul, Turkey,
was made entirely from other photographs.

## EDIBLE WOMAN

Do you recognize the woman made from fruits and vegetables in this portrait?

SEE PAGE 123 FOR THE SOLUTION AND ADDITIONAL INFORMATION.

## HUMAN STATUE OF LIBERTY

18,000 officers and enlisted men arrange themselves in a formation resembling the Statue of Liberty.

SEE PAGE 123 FOR ADDITIONAL INFORMATION.

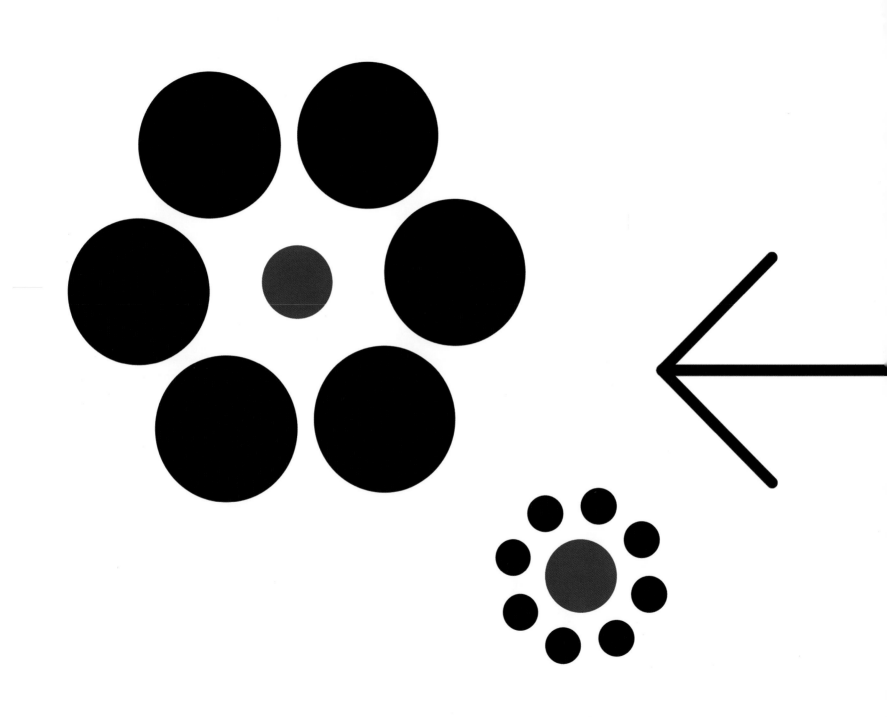

# ESTIMATION
## ILLUSIONS

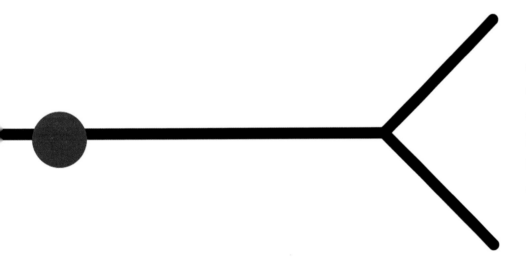

Estimation illusions are a common type of optical illusion that require the viewer to make assumptions about shapes, sizes, and lengths of various objects. Many of these effects were first discovered by researchers and psychologists in the late 19th century. Oftentimes, what is seen in these illusions and what is known to be true are in direct conflict. You may want to have a ruler or other straight-edge handy to help convince yourself that the correct answers are indeed correct.

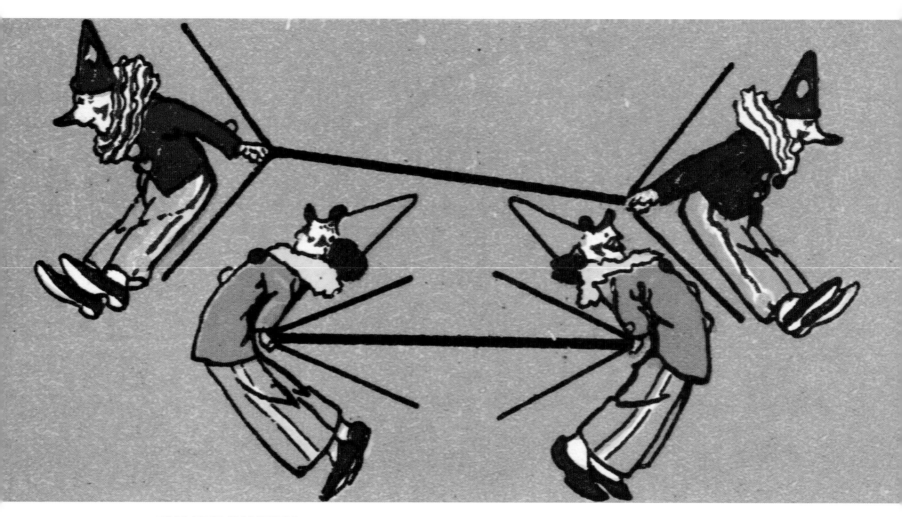

## THE ROD ILLUSION

Which is the longer of the two straight lines
stretching between the clowns' hands?

SEE PAGE 123 FOR THE SOLUTION AND ADDITIONAL INFORMATION.

## SKYSCRAPER ILLUSION

Do you think that the width of the skyscraper's base and its height (without the base) are equal?

SEE PAGE 124 FOR THE SOLUTION AND ADDITIONAL INFORMATION.

## ARCH ILLUSION

Which length of the Gateway Arch is greater, the width or the height?

SEE PAGE 124 FOR THE SOLUTION AND ADDITIONAL INFORMATION.

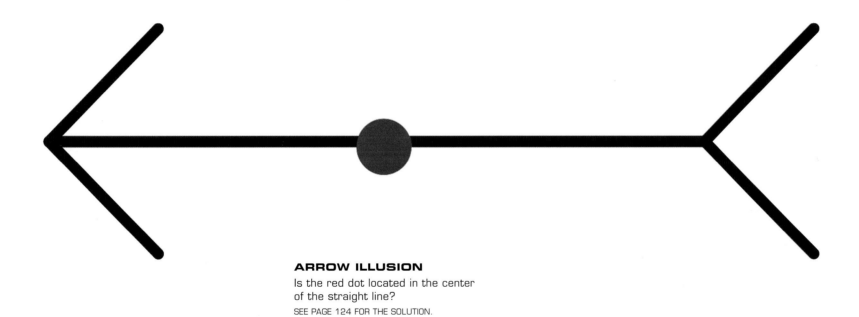

**ARROW ILLUSION**

Is the red dot located in the center
of the straight line?

SEE PAGE 124 FOR THE SOLUTION.

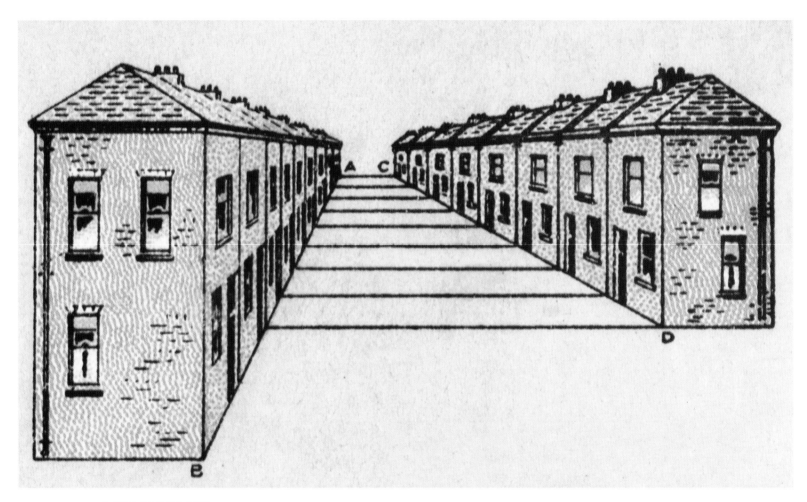

**LINE LENGTHS**

Which line is shorter, AB or CD?

SEE PAGE 124 FOR THE SOLUTION.

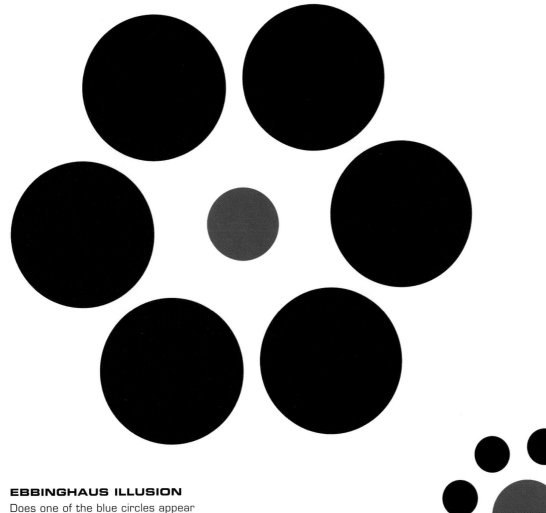

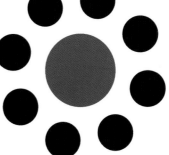

## EBBINGHAUS ILLUSION

Does one of the blue circles appear larger than the other?

SEE PAGE 124 FOR THE SOLUTION AND ADDITIONAL INFORMATION.

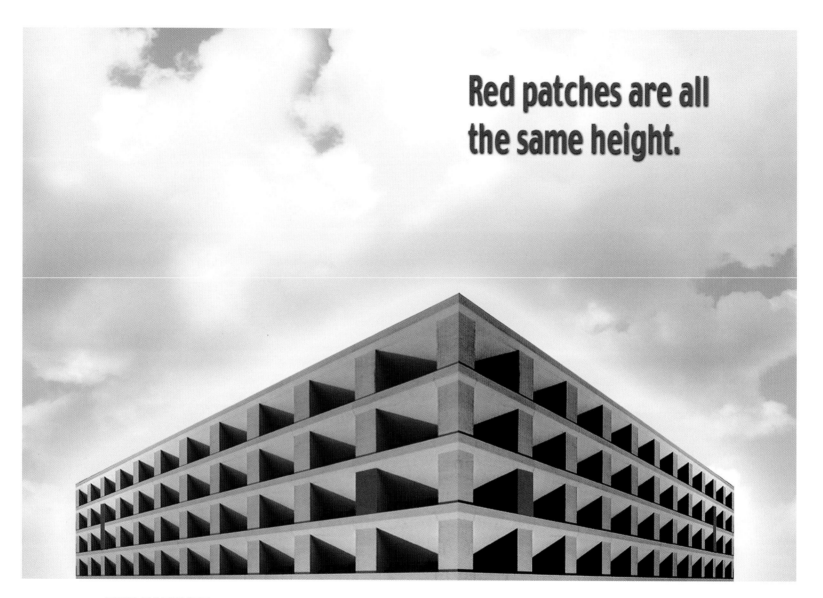

# Red patches are all the same height.

### RED PATCHES

As this graphic suggests, all of the red patches are the same height,
even though the outer patches appear to be significantly taller.

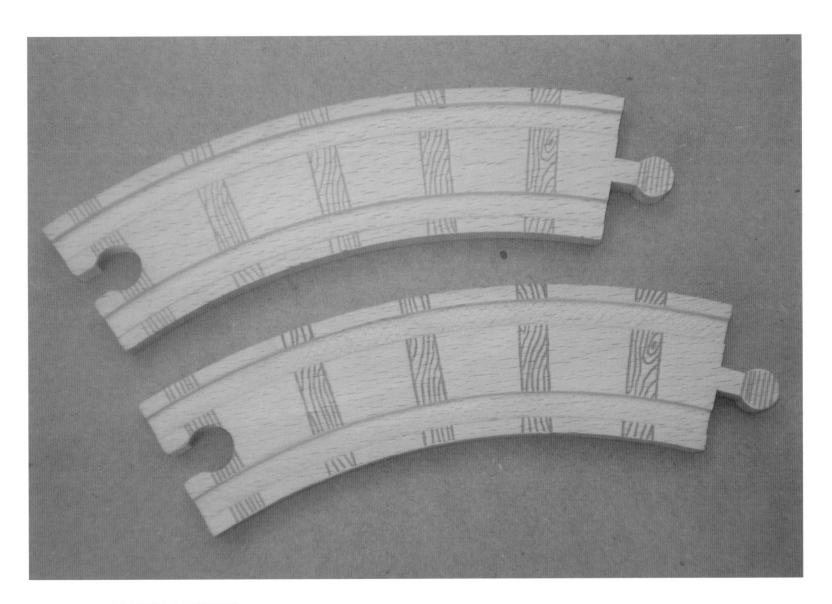

## TRACK ILLUSION

Which piece of train track is longer?

SEE PAGE 124 FOR THE SOLUTION AND ADDITIONAL INFORMATION.

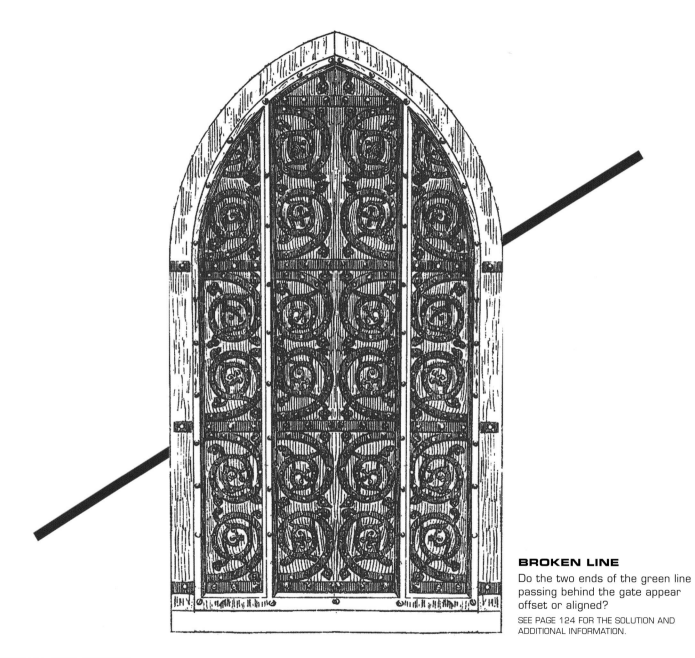

### BROKEN LINE

Do the two ends of the green line passing behind the gate appear offset or aligned?

SEE PAGE 124 FOR THE SOLUTION AND ADDITIONAL INFORMATION.

## BENT OR STRAIGHT?

This gate has two vertical bars toward the center. Are these bars bent or are they straight?

SEE PAGE 124 FOR THE SOLUTION AND ADDITIONAL INFORMATION.

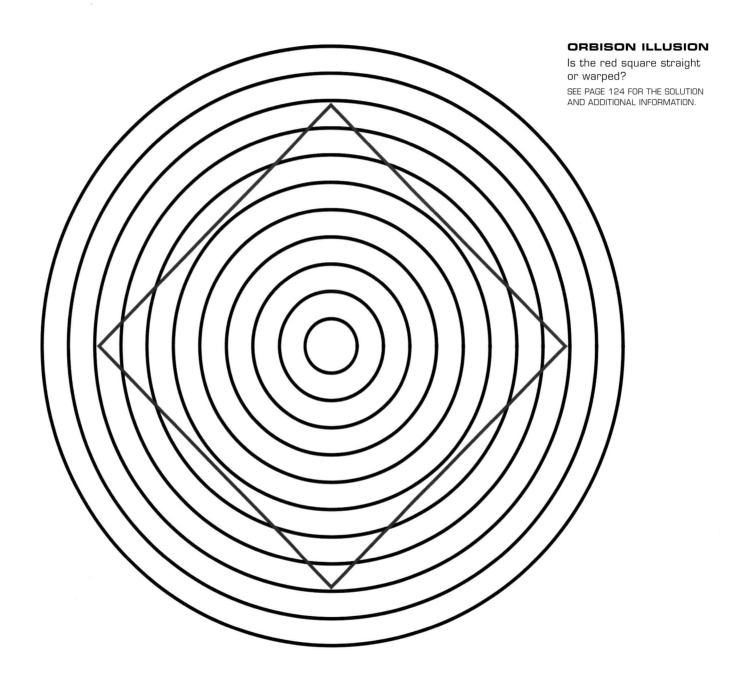

## ORBISON ILLUSION

Is the red square straight or warped?

SEE PAGE 124 FOR THE SOLUTION AND ADDITIONAL INFORMATION.

## CRAZY LETTERS

Are these letters perfectly upright and exactly parallel?

SEE PAGE 124 FOR THE SOLUTION AND ADDITIONAL INFORMATION.

# TROMPE L'OEIL
## ILLUSIONS

Trompe l'oeil (a French phrase meaning "to deceive the eye") is an art technique, often used on murals, that has been employed since ancient times. Art created using this method was an integral part of the culture of both the Greek and Roman Empires, and continues to amaze and confound to this day. It involves using extremely detailed imagery to trick viewers into thinking that the work itself is three-dimensional, and therefore real.

FOR EMMA, JOE ALICE & CLYDE

'Escape of the Mummy'

## ESCAPE OF THE MUMMY

3D chalk artist Tracy Lee Stum painted this 12' x 12' image on a flat surface for the 2008 Youth in Arts Italian Street Painting Festival in San Rafael, California. The painting depicts a mummy seemingly crawling out of a hole in the pavement, and took approximately 2-½ days to complete.

SEE PAGE 124 FOR ADDITIONAL INFORMATION.

## FLATIRON MURAL

Canadian artist Derek Michael Besant created the illusion of more windows than actually exist on the side of this building in Toronto, Ontario.

SEE PAGE 124 FOR ADDITIONAL INFORMATION.

## FULL GARAGE

It seems there is no room to park in the garage.
A design firm in Germany named style-your-garage.com
creates posters that can be affixed to garage doors
that trick people into thinking they are looking into
an open garage.

## TAYLOR HALL

Mural artist John Pugh makes it
appear that a flat wall has crumbled
to reveal a series of painted pillars.

SEE PAGE 124 FOR ADDITIONAL INFORMATION.

## MANSION WINDOWS

Only one of these windows is real. Can you tell which one it is?

SEE PAGE 124 FOR THE SOLUTION AND ADDITIONAL INFORMATION.

## READY FOR FLIGHT

A string coming out of the photograph taped to a wall gives the impression that this scene is three-dimensional.

## MOUSE TRAP

This interactive 3D street painting from Tracy Lee Stum was created for the 2010 Sarasota Chalk Festival in Florida. SEE PAGE 124 FOR ADDITIONAL INFORMATION.

### 3D LEGO TERRACOTTA ARMY

This 3D street art painting, designed by Leon Keer, was created for the 2011 Sarasota Chalk Festival in Sarasota, Florida. It measured 30 feet wide by 40 feet tall when completed. SEE PAGE 125 FOR ADDITIONAL INFORMATION.

# TOPSY-TURVY
## ILLUSIONS

Topsy-turvy illusions require the viewer to rotate the image to change the meaning or reveal some hidden imagery. In the late 19th and early 20th centuries, topsy-turvy images were commonly used as an amusing gimmick on advertisements and postcards. When viewed upside down, these images, which were frequently of human faces, would take on a new meaning.

**THE MYSTERIOUS ISLAND**

A small ship can be seen sailing past an opening in the rocks. Turning the picture upside down reveals a portrait of author Jules Verne. This topsy-turvy image was created by Hungarian artist István Orosz in 1979.

**ANOTHER FACE IN MOUNT RUSHMORE**

There are four faces clearly carved into the stone. Can you find a fifth face?

SEE PAGE 125 FOR THE SOLUTION AND ADDITIONAL INFORMATION.

vegas.

ambigram

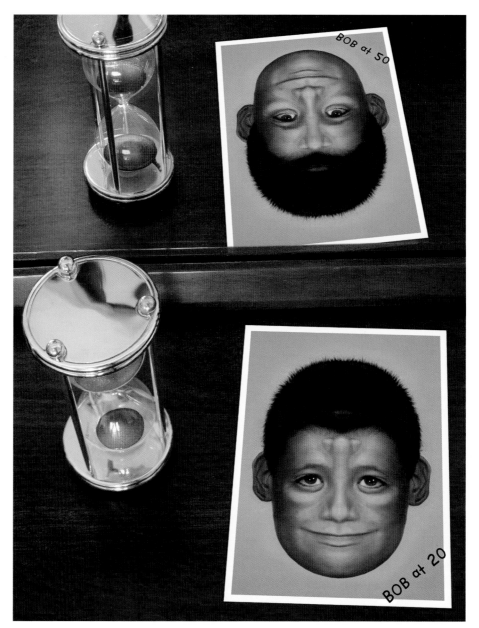

## LOOKING THROUGH TIME

The portrait reflected in the mirror shows an older version of the man seen in the portrait on the dresser.

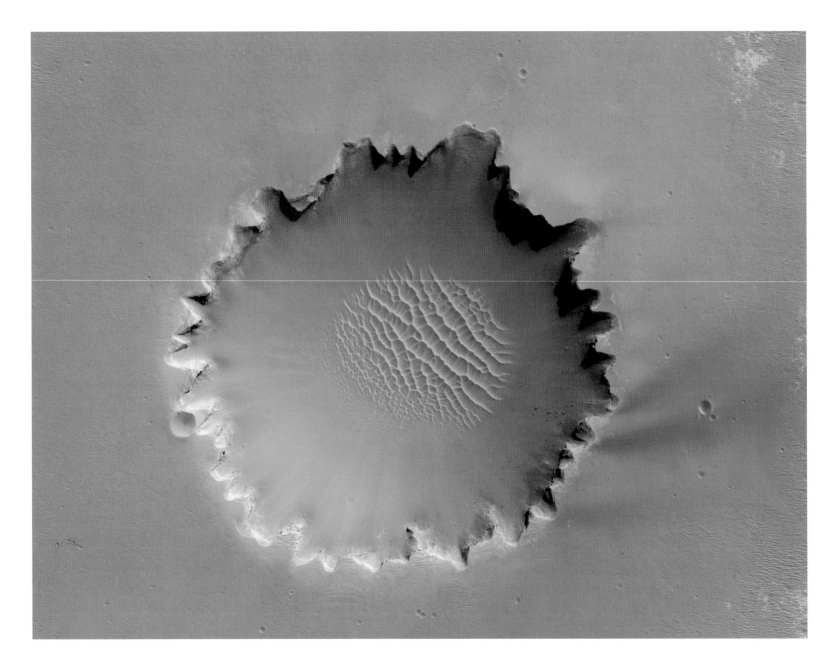

## VICTORIA CRATER

If you turn this page upside down, does the image still look like a crater?

SEE PAGE 125 FOR THE SOLUTION AND ADDITIONAL INFORMATION.

## BUSH ILLUSION

Can you tell what is wrong with this picture?

SEE PAGE 125 FOR THE SOLUTION AND ADDITIONAL INFORMATION.

**REVERSIBLE HEADS**

Rotate this image by 180 degrees
and sad faces become happy.

## THE GREENGROCER

A strange looking man wearing a helmet becomes a bowl full of vegetables when this image is turned upside down.

## UPSIDE DOWN HOUSE
### Exterior

This house, located in Trassenheide, Germany, features a completely upside down exterior and interior. Every room in the house, including the furniture, is completely inverted.

## UPSIDE DOWN HOUSE
### Interior

By turning a camera upside down, some very interesting gravity-defying photographs can be captured in this topsy-turvy structure.

UPSIDE DOWN
HEAD

This man's mood can
be changed by turning
his head upside down.

**A PUPPY AND ITS OWNER**

Turn this page upside down and the face
of a bearded man wearing a hat becomes
an adorable puppy with a bone.

# **NATURAL**
# ILLUSIONS

You do not always need to look far to find optical illusions. In fact, you can easily spot them by simply looking out a window. Rocks and clouds that resemble faces will cause you to do a double take. Natural phenomena such as the Northern Lights and colorful rainbows have dazzled humans for their entire existence.

## APACHE HEAD IN ROCKS

Do you see the head of a man formed in the rocks?

SEE PAGE 125 FOR THE SOLUTION AND ADDITIONAL INFORMATION.

## NORTHERN LIGHTS

This photograph of Aurora Borealis was captured above Bear Lake in Alaska.

SEE PAGE 125 FOR ADDITIONAL INFORMATION.

**WET ROAD**

Does this road look wet or dry?

SEE PAGE 125 FOR THE SOLUTION AND ADDITIONAL INFORMATION.

**MOON ILLUSION**

Does the moon appear to be unusually large in this photograph?

SEE PAGE 125 FOR THE SOLUTION AND ADDITIONAL INFORMATION.

**RAINBOW**

This beautiful illusion has been witnessed many times in the past.

SEE PAGE 125 FOR ADDITIONAL INFORMATION.

**LADY IN THE MOUNTAIN**

Do you see the profile of a woman's face in the mountain?

SEE PAGE 125 FOR ADDITIONAL INFORMATION.

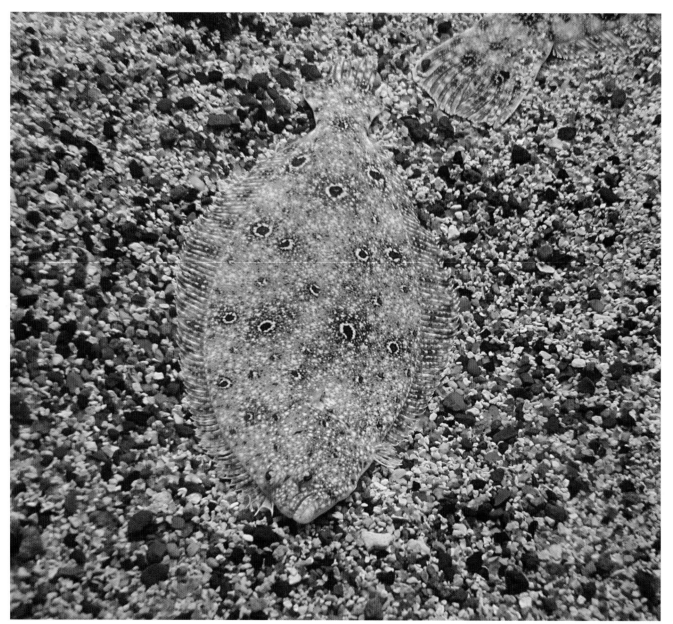

## NATURAL CAMOUFLAGE

Fish such as flounder can change their color and pattern to match their environment. This camouflage technique allows them to hide from hungry predators, thereby increasing their chances of survival.

## TRIANGULAR VOLCANO SHADOW

Why is the shadow of this volcano shaped like a triangle? The volcano itself is not an exact pyramid.

SEE PAGE 125 FOR THE SOLUTION AND ADDITIONAL INFORMATION.

# PERSPECTIVE
## ILLUSIONS

Sometimes illusions present themselves only from a specific viewing angle. Objects in the distance appear to be smaller than similarly sized objects in the foreground. Photographers and illustrators effectively use this trick to create works that seem to defy conventional logic.

## CLOUDS OF PEACE

By standing at the right angle, this photographer used passing clouds to give the impression that the cannon had recently been fired.

## WORLD'S TALLEST WALL?

Why would anyone build a wall this tall? And, more importantly, why would they need windows?

SEE PAGE 126 FOR THE SOLUTION AND ADDITIONAL INFORMATION.

**TILTED HOUSE**

Who would build a house like this?

SEE PAGE 126 FOR THE SOLUTION AND ADDITIONAL INFORMATION.

## HOLDING UP THE TOWER

Like many a tourist before him, this man takes a turn holding up the Leaning Tower of Pisa by taking the picture from the right angle.

## EUREKA TOWER CARPARK

Distorted letters on a parking lot wall can be read perfectly only when standing in
the right position. Viewing the letters from different angles reveals how the artist,
Axel Peemoeller, pulled off this incredible illusion. SEE PAGE 126 FOR ADDITIONAL INFORMATION.

## HOLDING THE SUN

A woman holds the sun between her fingers without getting burned.

## PAIR OF STAIRS

Do the two section of stairs appear parallel or skewed?

SEE PAGE 126 FOR THE SOLUTION AND ADDITIONAL INFORMATION.

## HOUSE I, 1998

This colorful house, designed by American pop artist Roy Lichtenstein, looks like a normal home from one vantage point. Moving to a different location, however, reveals that the structure is anything but ordinary. SEE PAGE 126 FOR ADDITIONAL INFORMATION.

## AMES ROOM

It appears that this man and his half-sized twin brother are standing side by side in the same room.

SEE PAGE 126 FOR THE SOLUTION AND ADDITIONAL INFORMATION.

## IMPOSSIBLE CRATE

Can you tell how this impossible crate was constructed?

SEE PAGE 126 FOR THE SOLUTION AND ADDITIONAL INFORMATION.

## PYRAMID FORCED PERSPECTIVE

Is this man really tall enough to touch the top of the Great Pyramid of Giza?

SEE PAGE 126 FOR THE SOLUTION AND ADDITIONAL INFORMATION.

## FEET ON THE MOON

The woman in this photograph may seem slender, but she has very strong legs.

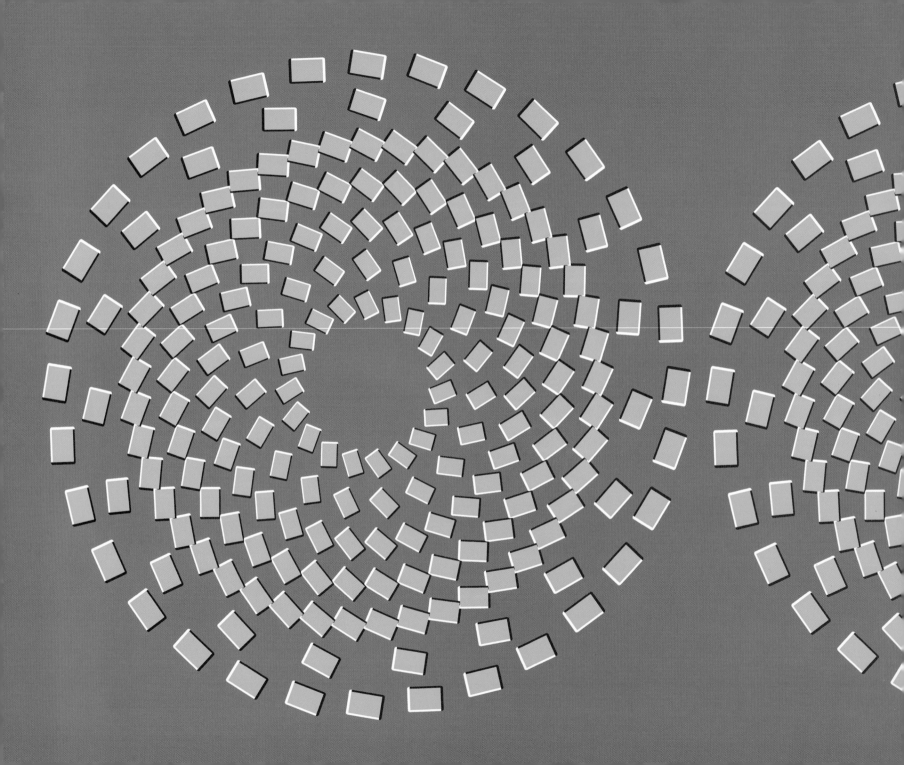

# MOTION
## ILLUSIONS

Motion illusions—also referred to as "anomalous motion illusions"—are static images that appear to move. Even though you know that a static image on a printed page cannot possibly move, your eyes and your brain still deceive you when the motion is perceived. This is a relatively new class of illusion with many new discoveries by vision researchers such as Akiyoshi Kitaoka of Ritsumeikan University in Kyoto, Japan, in the 21st century. Most of these illusions work best if you do not stare directly at them, but rather move your eyes rapidly around the entire image.

**WATERMELONS**

Do these watermelons appear to be rotating?

### STAR IN MOTION

Do you perceive this pattern to be moving in a counter-clockwise direction?

### REVOLVING WHEELS

Holding this vintage image level with your eyes, move it in small circles and the wheels will seem to revolve in the same direction.

SEE PAGE 126 FOR ADDITIONAL INFORMATION.

**ARROWS**

As you move your eyes around this image, do the arrows appear to separate from the rest of the figure and move?

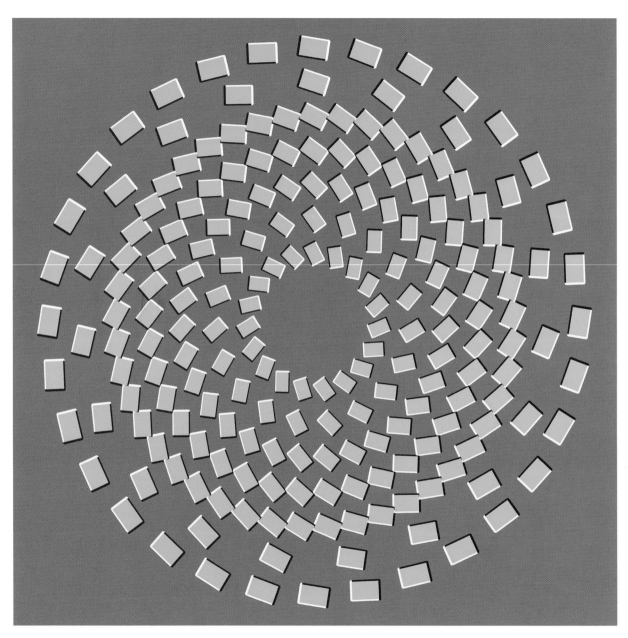

**GREEN BLOCKS**

Do the green blocks seem to be moving in a counter-clockwise direction as your eyes move around this image?

## PHANTOM ROTATION

Look at the circle in the center
and move your head toward and
then back away from the image.
The outer circles will appear to rotate.

SEE PAGE 126 FOR ADDITIONAL INFORMATION.

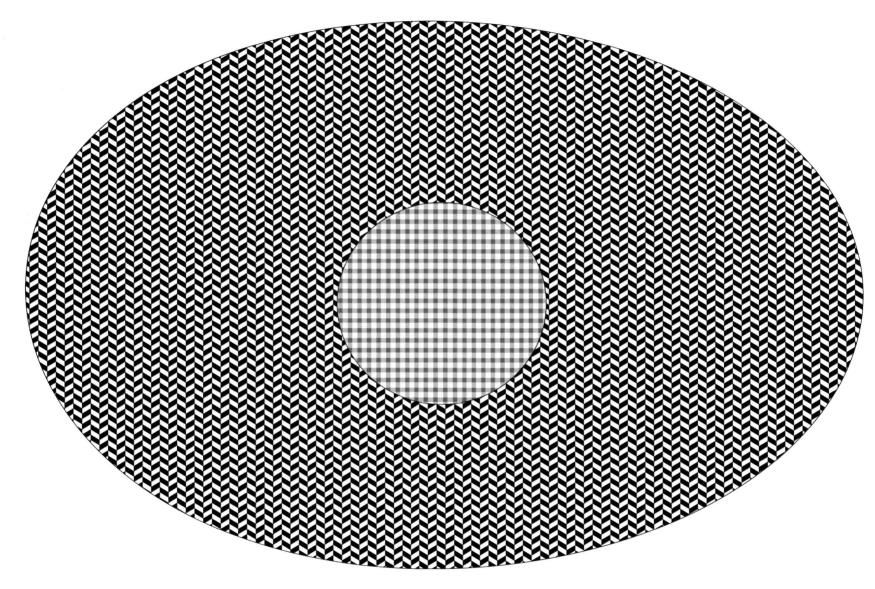

**MOVING EYE**

Stare at the circle in the center of this image. Does it seem to be unstable and move?

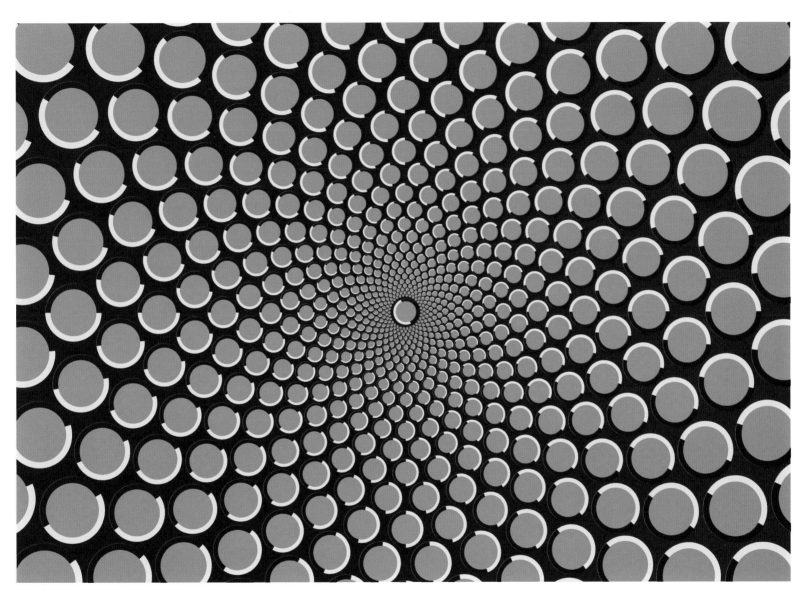

**GREEN CIRCLES**

Are the green circles rotating in a clockwise direction?

# **SOLUTIONS** AND ADDITIONAL INFORMATION

## AMBIGUOUS
## ILLUSIONS

### ANGEL COLUMNS

Page 12: David Barker created these unique columns in 1989 at Exploratorium, the San Francisco museum of science, art, and human perception. The spaces between the columns appear to be human figures. The columns were initially placed on a sidewall that received a lot of traffic. "I observed that people—mostly kids—would catch a glimpse of the shadowy angel figure from the corner of their eye. As they turned, they would see the illusion." Currently, the columns are located in the portico of the museum and continue to be a very popular exhibit.

### METAL PORTRAIT

Page 14: Metal Portraits (www.metalportraits. com) creates metal sculptures that are scaled to the size of a person's face. The result is a real-world example of an illusion that is known as the Rubin's vase illusion. Danish psychologist Edgar Rubin discovered this unique effect in the early 20th century.

### AMBIGUOUS CHEESE

Page 15: Both interpretations are correct, depending on how you look at this image. At first glance, most people seem to see a slab of cheese with a section cut from it.

### I GOT A DEER

Page 16: The negative space in the lion's mouth resembles the head of a small deer.

### THE GHOST IN THE TOWER

Page 17: A sinister face appears to hover between the two women toasting glasses of wine. Metamorphic drawings such as this one were very popular on postcards and advertisements during the latter part of the 19th century.

### NEGATIVE SPACE AMBIGRAM

Page 18: The word ALIVE can be seen in the red lettering. In the white space between the red letters, the word DEAD can also be found. This figure/ground ambigram was designed by Nikita Prokhorov, a graphic designer who co-owns and writes for www.ambigram.com, the largest ambigram community website in the world.

### PERCEIVED OBJECTS

Page 19: Although this image does not contain a triangle and a sphere, most people perceive both of them in the white space between the black objects.

### ERNEST HEMINGWAY

Page 20: The black portions of this illustration form the tip of a fountain pen.

### MAD OR SAD?

Page 23: If you are having trouble locating both faces, the sad man is looking up and to the right, and the mad man is looking down and to the left.

## IMPOSSIBLE
## ILLUSIONS

### IMPOSSIBLE TRIANGLE

Page 28: The triangle depicted in this photograph could not actually exist in nature, but this is a real sculpture located in a campground in Gotschuchen, Austria. The sculpture consists of three bars angled in such a way that when viewed from a specific location, it appears to be a triangle that is "impossible."

### HIGHWAY

Page 29: This image is part of Michael Kai's "This Side Up" series, which features a collection of photographs with perspectives that are impossible. The remaining images, which are equally as stunning, can be viewed on his website at www.michaelkai.net.

### IMPOSSIBLE NUTS

Page 30: It is obvious that this straight bar could not pass through the two nuts. But if that were true, then how was this picture taken? The nuts are constructed inside-out, but appear normal when viewed from a certain angle. The holes do not face opposite directions, as the photograph would suggest, allowing a straight bar to pass through. This illusion was constructed by magician Jerry Andrus.

### IMPOSSIBLE SPIRAL STAIRCASE

Page 31: It would take a long time to walk up this spiral staircase. If you follow the staircase, it appears that as you try to climb up the stairs, you end up descending.

### TOURIST TRAP II

Page 33: Erwin Bonsma took inspiration from M.C. Escher's "Concave and Convex" when designing this image. He further wished to note the following credits: the image was rendered using the POVRay raytracer; the grass was made using macros by Gilles Tran; the palm tree was made using a tree macro by Tom Aust and modified by Gena Obukhov; the chain was made using a macro by the PM 2Ring with catenary calculations by Zdislav Kovarik.

### BELT

Page 37: Swedish multimedia artist Andreas Aronsson designs impossible figures using a variety of software programs. His designs typically have a three-dimensional perspective and present perplexing objects and structures.

## COMPOSITE
## ILLUSIONS

### SUMMER

Page 42: Giuseppe Arcimboldo painted this composite portrait in 1563. Arcimboldo, an Italian painter from the 16th century, painted many portraits of people from collected objects including fruits, vegetables, flowers, fish, and books, among others.

### PIXEL PRESIDENT

Page 43: American artist Scott Blake created this unique series of composite images. He began by arranging the portraits according to their grayscale density. Portraits containing dark ties and hair were used to fill in the dark areas, while the lighter areas were filled by presidents who wore lighter clothing or had light-colored (or no) hair. More of this artist's work can be viewed at www.barcodeart.com.

### POST-IT NOTE ELVIS

Page 44: From a distance, this portrait of Elvis is even more recognizable.

### EDIBLE WOMAN

Page 46: It is Mona Lisa. This composite image was created using Dynamic Auto-Painter by MediaChance. This program will automatically turn an image into a painting inspired by some of the most famous artists in the world.

### HUMAN STATUE OF LIBERTY

Page 47: This photograph was taken at Camp Dodge in Des Moines, Iowa, during a promotional campaign to sell war bonds during World War I, but was never used. The photograph was taken by Mole & Thomas, a studio in Chicago, from the top of a large tower constructed for the purposes of capturing this shot. Many men fainted during the photo shoot as a result of wearing woolen uniforms in temperatures nearing 105 degrees F. Due to the fact that it is the greatest distance away from the camera, 12,000 of the 18,000 men in this photo-graph are standing in the flame of the torch.

## ESTIMATION
## ILLUSIONS

### THE ROD ILLUSION

Page 50: Using a ruler, you will find that both lines are exactly the same size. The presence of the angled lines at either end of the lines gives the impression that the top line is longer. This illusion is a variation of the Müller-Lyer illusion first discovered in 1889.

## SKYSCRAPER ILLUSION

Page 51: Both are the same length, although the height of the building certainly appears longer than the width of the base.

## ARCH ILLUSION

Page 52: While it looks taller than it is wide, both the width and height of the Gateway Arch in St. Louis, Missouri, are the same: 630 feet. The Gateway Arch was completed in 1965 and is the tallest man-made monument in the United States.

## ARROW ILLUSION

Page 53: While it appears to be left of center, the red dot is in the exact middle of the line on this arrow.

## LINE LENGTHS

Page 54: Lines AB and CD are both the same length. The steeper angle of line CD gives it the appearance of being shorter than AB.

## EBBINGHAUS ILLUSION

Page 55: The blue circles are the exact same size. Most viewers perceive the circle surrounded by the smaller circles to be larger than the circle surrounded by the bigger circles. Hermann Ebbinghaus, a German psychologist, discovered this relative size visual perception effect in the late 19th century.

## TRACK ILLUSION

Page 57: Although the bottom track appears longer than the upper track, they are identical in size. This illusion was discovered by American psychologist Joseph Jastrow during the late 19th century.

## BROKEN LINE

Page 58: The two ends of the line are completely aligned, although they appear to be offset. German physicist Johann Christian Poggendorff discovered this illusion in 1860.

## BENT OR STRAIGHT?

Page 59: The bars are perfectly straight and parallel with the frame of the gate even though they appear to bow outward. This illusion is known as the Hering illusion, and was named for the German psychologist, Ewald Hering, who was first described in 1861.

## ORBISON ILLUSION

Page 60: Despite appearances, the square is not warped at all. If you need proof, measure each side with a straight edge. Psychologist William Orbison discovered this optical effect in 1939.

## CRAZY LETTERS

Page 61: All three letters are upright and parallel to one another. The thick, angled lines within the letters deceive the eye as to the true shape of the letters.

# TROMPE L'OEIL ILLUSIONS

## ESCAPE OF THE MUMMY

Page 64: The artist found inspiration from Indiana Jones and the Mummy while composing this painting. More 3D street paintings from Tracy Lee Stum can be found at her website at www.tracyleestum.com.

## FLATIRON MURAL

Page 65: This mural, completed in 1980, was commissioned by the City of Toronto Public Art, and is made from more than 50 panels that mounted on a steel frame. It measures 26' wide by 46' tall.

## TAYLOR HALL

Page 67: This mural is located on Taylor Hall at California State University, in Chico, California. It has become a popular visitor attraction and landmark in downtown Chico. Shortly after this mural was completed, a woman who worked across the street from Taylor Hall called the administration to find out when they planned to fix the hole in the wall.

## MANSION WINDOWS

Page 68: The only real window in this photograph is the top one on the right. The rest are painted on the side of this building located in Alpes-Maritimes, France.

## MOUSE TRAP

Page 70: This painting measures 65' x 30' and took approximately 3-½ days to complete. Due to the limited time available to create the painting, the artist recruited four friends/ street painters to assist with this enormous project. Both chalk and non-permanent paint were used.

### 3D LEGO TERRACOTTA ARMY

Page 71: The 2011 Sarasota Chalk Festival was the 4th season of the annual week-long cultural event and attracted over 200,000 visitors. The artist took inspiration from the Terracotta Army of Qin Shi Huang, the first emperor of China. Ruben Poncia, Remko van Schaik and Peter Westerink assisted in the creation of this painting.

# TOPSY-TURVY ILLUSIONS

### ANOTHER FACE IN MOUNT RUSHMORE

Page 75: If you rotate the book counter-clockwise by 90 degrees, the rock formation itself looks like another face. The Mount Rushmore National Memorial, located near Keystone, South Dakota, was created as a way to promote tourism in the area.

### AMBIGRAMS

Page 76: Ambigrams mix illusion and symmetry to create art that presents two or more words in the same physical space. These two examples are rotational ambigrams that show the same word when read normally or upside down. Two American artists, Scott Kim and John Langdon, are generally credited for being responsible for the popularization of this art form.

### VICTORIA CRATER

Page 78: This is a photograph from NASA of an impact crater near the equator of Mars. When most people view a concave image like this upside down, it appears to be convex.

### BUSH ILLUSION

Page 79: When you turn the book upside down, it should be obvious. His mouth and eyes have been inverted but it is difficult to tell when the face is upside down. This effect was originally discovered by Peter Thompson, a professor at the University of York, using a picture of former British Prime Minister Margaret Thatcher. As such, it is often called the Thatcher illusion.

# NATURAL ILLUSIONS

### APACHE HEAD IN ROCKS

Page 88: This incredible natural illusion can be seen in Ebihens, France. The green foliage even seems to form a full head of hair, further enhancing the illusion.

### NORTHERN LIGHTS

Page 89: Eskimos had many legends about the cause of the Northern Lights, believing that they were supernatural. The real cause is the collision between particles from the sun and gases in the Earth's atmosphere.

### WET ROAD

Page 90: The road is completely dry. This photograph was taken on a hot, sunny day. The "wet spots" on the road are actually a naturally occurring mirage caused by bent light rays, making the sky appear to reflect off of the road's surface.

### MOON ILLUSION

Page 91: The photographer, Gordon Gillet, took this photograph from a distance of approximately 8½ miles. The moon appears to be extremely large in this photograph because it is seen close to the horizon, and the objects on the ground distort our perception of its relative size.

### RAINBOW

Page 92: Mother Nature was generating this illusion long before humans were around to appreciate it. This photographer was lucky enough to capture a double rainbow.

### LADY IN THE MOUNTAIN

Page 93: This picture was taken in the Bay of Islands, a popular fishing, sailing, and tourist destination in New Zealand.

### TRIANGULAR VOLCANO SHADOW

Page 94: This triangle shadow phenomena is frequently seen from the tops of large mountains and volcanoes, and is caused because the viewer is looking at a shadow that extends to the horizon. This shadow has the appearance of tapering off because the shadow extends so far away from the viewer. A similar angled effect can be seen by looking down a long set of parallel train tracks. This particular photograph was taken on Tenerife in the Canary Islands of Spain.

# PERSPECTIVE
## ILLUSIONS

### WORLD'S TALLEST WALL?

Page 99: This is a photograph of the Nix Professional Building in San Antonio, Texas. The 23-story building has an angled corner, that, when viewed from a specific perspective, creates the illusion of a flat wall. At any other angle, the true shape of the building is obvious.

### TILTED HOUSE

Page 100: This house is built on a steep hill and the photograph was taken with the camera parallel to the road.

### EUREKA TOWER CARPARK

Page 102: The artist designed these letters while working for Emery Studio. This project won several international design awards.

### PAIR OF STAIRS

Page 105: This is the exact same photograph presented side by side, yet the stairs do not seem parallel. The set of stairs on the left seem to be at a much sharper angle than the

set on the right. This illusion is also known as the "Leaning Tower Illusion," and was discovered by Frederick Kingdom, Ali Yoonessi, and Elena Gheorghiu of McGill University. In 2007, their variation of this illusion won first prize at the Best Illusion of the Year Contest.

### HOUSE I, 1998

Page 106: This sculpture is made of fabricated and painted aluminum. It is located in the Sculpture Garden of the National Gallery of Art in Washington, DC.

### AMES ROOM

Page 108: This photograph is an example of an Ames room, a room that is constructed such that the room appears to be a cube when viewed from a certain vantage point. In reality, the back wall is slanted, with one side much farther from the viewer than the other, which gives the impression that the person standing near the wall closest to the viewer is much bigger than the person standing farther away. The accompanying illustration further demonstrates how an Ames room works.

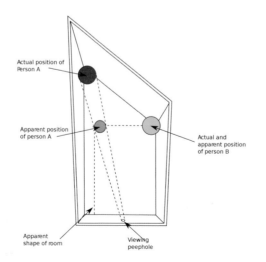

Actual position of Person A

Apparent position of person A

Actual and apparent position of person B

Apparent shape of room

Viewing peephole

### IMPOSSIBLE CRATE

Page 109: The solution to the construction of this impossible crate is presented on the image below. The crate only appears to be impossible when viewed from a specific angle. Magician Jerry Andrus created this amusing and perplexing exhibit.

### PYRAMID FORCED PERSPECTIVE

Page 110: Since the Great Pyramid of Giza in Egypt is nearly 480 feet tall, the answer should be fairly obvious. He can only appear tall enough to do so if the photograph is taken from the right angle.

## MOTION ILLUSIONS

### REVOLVING WHEELS

Page 116: Illustrations like this one that utilize the revolving wheel illusion, were used on a number of postcards and advertisements during the late 19th and early 20th centuries.

### PHANTOM ROTATION

Page 119: This illusion was proposed by Baingio Pinna and G. Brelstaff in 2000. As such, it is often referred to as the Pinna illusion.

# ACKNOWLEDGMENTS

SPECIAL THANKS are extended to Jeanine DeNoma from Friends of Jerry Andrus (www.jerryandrus.org), Alan Gottlieb (www.Oldpostcards.com & www.UStownviews.com), and Terry Stickels (www.terrystickels.com).

Pages 6, 7, and 108: Copyright Alvaho/Fred van Houten, www.digitalvaho.com
Page 9: Copyright Roger N. Shepard from the book Mind Sights (1990, W.H. Freeman)
Pages 10, 11, 13, 16, 24, 25, and 36: Copyright Chow Hon Lam aka Flying Mouse, www.flyingmouse365.com
Page 12: Copyright Exploratorium/Courtesy of David Barker
Page 14: Courtesy of www.metalportraits.com
Page 17: Courtesy of www.oldpostcards.com and www.ustownviews.com
Page 18: Copyright Nikita Prokhorov, www.elusiveillusion.com
Pages 20 and 27: Copyright Tang Yau Hoong, www.tangyauhoong.com
Pages 22, 26, and back cover (center): Copyright Gianni A. Sarcone, www.archimedes-lab.org
Page 23: Copyright Humberto Machado
Page 29: Copyright Michael Kai, www.michaelkai.net
Pages 30, 109, and 126 (far right): Copyright Jerry Andrus/ Courtesy of George Andrus
Page 31: Copyright Toshiyuki Akanuma
Page 32: Copyright Tamás Farkas, www.farkas-tamas.hu
Page 33: Copyright Erwin Bonsma
Page 34: Copyright Robbert van der Steeg
Pages 35, 38, 39, 45, and back cover (left): Courtesy of Nevit Dilmen
Page 37: Copyright Andreas Aronsson, www.andreasaronsson.com
Page 40: Copyright Boris A. Glazer, www.mazaika.com
Page 41: Copyright Ken Knowlton, www.kenknowlton.com
Page 43: Copyright Scott Blake, www.BarcodeArt.com

Pages 44 and 123: Copyright Charles Mangin
Pages 46, 57, and 58: Copyright Brad Honeycutt, www.bradhoneycutt.com
Pages 51 and 56: Copyright Gene Levine, www.colorstereo.com
Pages 62, 63, and 70: Courtesy of Michael Moore Photography
Page 64: Photograph by Joy Phoenix/Courtesy of www.youthinarts.org
Page 65: Copyright Derek Michael Besant, www.derekbesant.com
Page 66: Courtesy of www.style-your-garage.com
Page 67 and back cover (right): Copyright John Pugh, www.artofjohnpugh.com
Page 69: Copyright Iskren Semkov
Page 71: Copyright Leon Keer, www.streetpainting3d.com
Pages 72, 73, and 80: Copyright Paul Howalt, www.paulhowalt.com
Page 74: Copyright István Orosz, utisz.blogspot.com
Page 77: Copyright Robert Fathauer, www.tessellations.com
Page 79: Photo manipulation by Don Ebert
Pages 82 and 83: Courtesy of www.weltstehtkopf.de
Page 85: Copyright Valentine Dubinin, www.valdub.ru
Pages 86, 87, and 91: Courtesy of G. Gillet/ESO
Page 92: Courtesy of Andrew McMillan
Page 93: Copyright Bill Bishofberger
Page 94: Copyright C. Frank Starmer
Page 95: Copyright Juan Carlos Casado, www.starryearth.com
Page 98: Copyright Giulia Piu
Pages 99 and 126 (far left): Copyright Jason Sousa
Page 101: Courtesy of www.panoptikum.net
Pages 102 and 103: Courtesy of Axel Peemoeller, www.axelpeemoeller.com
Page 105: Photograph Copyright Wladyslaw Sojka
Pages 106 and 107: Sculpture Copyright Estate of Roy Lichtenstein/ Photograph Copyright Karen Katz
Page 111: Copyright Laurent Laveder, www.pixheaven.net
Pages 112, 113, and 118: Copyright Jaime Vives Piqueres, www.ignorancia.org
Pages 114 and 117: Copyright Miwa Miwa
Pages 115, 121, and front cover: Copyright Fiestoforo, www.fiestoforo.cl
Page 120: Copyright Anh Pham, www.anhphamillusion.co.cc

# INDEX

## ABOUT THE AUTHOR

BRAD HONEYCUTT is a web developer, author, and optical illusion enthusiast. He is the co-author of *The Art of the Illusion: Deceptions to Challenge the Eye and the Mind* and creative advisor for *Startling Stereograms* (both Imagine/Charlesbridge, 2012), and has worked extensively with two of the world's leading stereogram creators to help publish books containing their 3-D creations. Brad currently operates www.anopticalillusion.com, a website updated with a new optical illusion each and every weekday. He holds a Bachelor of Arts degree from Michigan State University, where he graduated with high honors.